BARENTS SEA

RUSSIA

...orld.
...on ...
for another
3,750 miles!
(6035 km)

URAL MOUNTAINS

1 Votkinsk ●

2 ● St. Petersburg

3 Moscow ★

UKRAINE

4 ● Brailov

TO THE USA   N   TO RUSSIA
W ●─ E
S

ENGLAND   London
Paris ●   Berlin ●
FRANCE   GERMANY
AUSTRIA   Vienna ●

ITALY

MEDITERRANEAN SEA   Rome

5

TIMELINE OF PETER TCHAIKOVSKY'S LIFE

1840 Peter Tchaikovsky is born in Votkinsk, Russia.

1844 Four-year-old Peter shows an interest in music. He writes a simple song for his mom.

1845 Peter starts piano lessons.

1848 The Tchaikovsky family moves to St. Petersburg, where Peter enters boarding school.

1850 Peter Tchaikovsky enters a school in St. Petersburg where he studies law and joins the school choir. After nine years, he graduates and begins a job as a law clerk.

1862 -1863 Peter finds he is much more interested in music than a career in law. He enrolls in the new St. Petersburg Music Conservatory and quits his job.

1866 Peter moves to Moscow to study and teach music at the new Moscow Conservatory.

1868 -1874 Tchaikovsky keeps busy writing music, including his Symphony No. 1.

THIS WAY

UP HERE

1875 Tchaikovsky begins writing his first ballet, *Swan Lake*.

1876 Peter begins a friendship with the wealthy Nadezhda von Meck. Nadezhda offers to support Peter so he can write music without money worries.

1877 Peter Tchaikovsky marries Antonina Milyukova. The marriage turns out to be a big mistake, and they separate after only two months.

1880 -1890 Tchaikovsky travels all over Europe and Russia. He composes dozens of new pieces, including two symphonies and the *Sleeping Beauty* ballet.

1891 Peter tours the United States for the first time.

1892 *The Nutcracker* ballet opens in St. Petersburg.

1893 In October, Peter Tchaikovsky conducts the premiere of his final symphony, Symphony No. 6. Just a few weeks later, he becomes ill with a serious stomach problem. Peter dies on November 6 in St. Petersburg.

GETTING TO KNOW
THE WORLD'S
GREATEST COMPOSERS

PETER
TCHAIKOVSKY

WRITTEN AND ILLUSTRATED BY MIKE VENEZIA

CONSULTANT
DONALD FREUND, PROFESSOR OF COMPOSITION,
INDIANA UNIVERSITY SCHOOL OF MUSIC

CHILDREN'S PRESS®

An Imprint of Scholastic Inc.

*To my grade-school, high-school, and college teachers—
the good ones who made a difference.*

Picture Acknowledgements
Photos ©: cover and title page: Stock Montage; 3: North Wind Picture Archives; 6: Gjon Mili/
Getty Images; 7 top: Aaron Chown/AP Images; 7 bottom: Alexandr Kryazhev/AP Images;
12-13: Heritage Images/Getty Images; 20-21: Russian State Museum, St. Petersburg,
Russia/Scala/Art Resource, NY; 23: Stock Montage; 30: UniversalImagesGroup/Getty Images;
31: Nigel Norrington/AP Images; 32: Costas; 33-34: Stock Montage.

Library of Congress Cataloging-in-Publication Data

Names: Venezia, Mike, author, illustrator.
Title: Peter Tchaikovsky / written and illustrated by Mike Venezia ;
    consultant, Donald Freund.
Description: Revised edition. | New York, NY : Children's Press, 2018. |
    Series: Getting to know the world's greatest composers | Includes
    bibliographical references and index.
Identifiers: LCCN 2017048082| ISBN 9780531228685 (library binding) | ISBN
    9780531233719 (pbk.)
Subjects: LCSH: Tchaikovsky, Peter Ilich, 1840-1893--Juvenile literature. |
    Composers--Russia--Biography--Juvenile literature.
Classification: LCC ML3930.C4 V46 2018 | DDC 780.92 [B] --dc23 LC record available at
https://lccn.loc.gov/2017048082

All rights reserved. Published in 2018 by Children's Press, an imprint of Scholastic Inc.
Printed in North Mankato, MN, USA 113

Scholastic Inc., 557 Broadway, New York, NY 10012.

1 2 3 4 5 6 7 8 9 10 R 27 26 25 24 23 22 21 20 19 18

Peter Ilyich Tchaikovsky

Peter Tchaikovsky was born in the Russian town of Votkinsk in 1840. He used his great imagination to create beautiful music that was sometimes very happy and sometimes very sad.

$\mathbf{P}$eter wrote his music during a time known as the Romantic period. The music written by Romantic composers wasn't necessarily about falling in love—

but about their own dream world and deepest feelings. When you listen to Peter Tchaikovsky's music, you can often tell how he felt while he was writing it.

A scene from *Swan Lake*, as performed by the New York City Ballet

Romantic composers sometimes wrote their music to go along with a well-known story or poem. Tchaikovsky's three ballets, *Swan Lake*, *Sleeping Beauty*, and *The Nutcracker*, all came from popular stories.

A scene from *The Nutcracker*, as performed by
the Birmingham Royal Ballet in England

A scene from *Sleeping Beauty*, as performed by the
Novosibirsk Opera and Ballet Theater in Russia

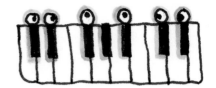

Peter Tchaikovsky first became interested in music when he was four or five years old. One day, Peter's father brought home an orchestrion, a machine that played music. It was like a giant music box with lots of additional parts, so it sounded more like a real orchestra.

One of the pieces the orchestrion played was a tune by Wolfgang Amadeus Mozart. He was a famous Austrian composer who had lived during the 1700s, before Peter was born.

Peter loved Mozart's music. He tried to
copy the pieces he heard from the orchestrion
on his family's piano.

While Peter was growing up, he was very sensitive. Things that wouldn't bother most children seemed like the worst thing in the world to Peter.

Being supersensitive was always a problem for Peter Tchaikovsky, but it was also one of the reasons he was able to write such beautiful music.

Peter had feelings about things that most people didn't even think about. He was able to put those feelings into his music.

As a young man, Peter Tchaikovsky didn't start out to become a serious composer. Even though he wrote some pieces and played the piano and flute pretty well, music was really more of a hobby than a career. At the time when Peter was growing up, hardly anyone in Russia made a living by writing music.

In fact, Peter's parents had always planned for him to become a lawyer. When he was ten years old, his parents decided he should begin learning about law. They sent him to a few different schools in St. Petersburg, the city where they lived.

St. Petersburg in 1803

When Peter was twenty-one, he graduated from law school, and took a job in a government office.

During Peter's time, when it came to serious classical music, people in Russia were satisfied listening to the music of composers from Italy, France, Austria, Germany, and other parts of Europe.

Fortunately for Peter, things were starting to change in Russia. There was a group of people in St. Petersburg who thought it was about time that Russia had its own music, written by Russia's own composers.

Soon after Peter started his job, a new music school opened up in St. Petersburg. Since music was practically all Peter could think about, and since he didn't really like

his job that much, he thought it might be a
good time to quit and start studying music
seriously at the new school.

One of Peter's teachers at the school was a famous musician named Anton Rubinstein. Anton knew Peter could become a great composer someday, and worked hard with him to develop his talents. Later, when Anton's equally famous brother, Nikolai, started a new music school in the city of Moscow, Peter was invited to join him as a teacher. Peter was able to make a small

salary while continuing to learn about music from Nikolai.

Both Anton and Nikolai were very tough on Peter. They often criticized his music as a way of making sure Peter was doing the best work he could. Although Peter didn't like to be criticized, he learned a lot from the two brothers, and ended up becoming friends with them.

It wasn't long before Peter Tchaikovsky started to do very well with his music. Once, he was asked to conduct one of his pieces for an audience. Peter was so nervous, he imagined his head might fall off, and held tightly to his beard through the entire performance.

It took ten years before Peter felt he could conduct in front of an audience again.

Peter was always getting upset about things that were completely imaginary.

Peter worked so hard on his music that he sometimes made himself sick. When he was writing his first symphony, he worked night and day until he wore himself out trying to get it just the way he wanted. Peter named his first symphony *Winter Dreams*. When you listen to it, you can almost see wintry fields, and imagine the feeling of riding a horse-drawn sleigh over the snowy Russian countryside that Peter

Carnival of 1916, a wintry Russian
landscape by Boris Kustodiev

loved so much. *Winter Dreams* (also called
Symphony No. 1 in G Minor) is a good
example of how Peter Tchaikovsky was
able to put what he felt or dreamt about
into music.

Peter also included melodies from Russian folk songs in his first symphony. He had always enjoyed listening to folk songs when he was little.

Peter listened carefully when he heard working people whistling outside his window or children singing while playing in the streets. He wrote down some of these folk tunes, and used them in his later symphonies, operas, and ballets.

Many Romantic composers got musical ideas from their country's folk songs and peasant dances. Composers like Franz Liszt,

An 1800 engraving of Russian
peasants doing traditional folk dances

Frédéric Chopin, Edvard Grieg, and Nikolai
Rimsky-Korsakov all used folk music to add
excitement to their music and show how
proud they were of their countries and their
histories.

By the time Peter was thirty-seven years old, he had written three operas, three symphonies, one ballet, and lots of other musical pieces. Sometimes his music was well liked, but many times, people didn't care for it at all. Peter was upset by this as well as by the fact that he wasn't making very much money.

Just when Peter was starting to worry about his future, an amazing thing happened! A rich widow who loved Peter's music decided to help him out. Madam Nadezhda von Meck wanted Peter to be able to work on his music without worrying about money or having to get another job.

She agreed to give Peter money every year, as long as they would never meet each other face to face. Peter went along with Madam von Meck's wishes, and as strange as it seems, they became best friends by writing each other letters for many years. In fact, Peter dedicated his famous Symphony No. 4 in F Minor to Madam von Meck.

Peter Tchaikovsky had always loved to travel. Now that he had more money, he felt better about taking trips all over Europe. He sometimes gave concerts in the cities he visited. His travels also gave him ideas for new music.

Peter was very close to his family, especially his brother, Modeste, and his sister, Sasha. Peter often traveled with Modeste.

On one trip to Paris, France, Peter heard a newly invented instrument called a celesta. It looked like a small piano, but made a beautiful bell-like sound.

Peter thought it would be a perfect instrument to add to his new *Nutcracker* suite. Peter wanted to be the first composer to use the celesta, and had one secretly smuggled out of Paris. You can hear its magical bell-like sound throughout the "Dance of the Sugar Plum Fairy."

One of Peter Tchaikovsky's talents was discovering new instruments, and using unusual new combinations of instruments to get beautiful and exciting sounds into his music.

In one of his most famous pieces, the *1812 Overture*, Peter even used church bells and real cannons to get just the right sound.

Peter Tchaikovsky

Even though Peter Tchaikovsky became famous all over the world for his music, he was very unhappy much of the time. One of his biggest problems was that he could never find the right person to fall in love with. Peter felt like he was missing out on one of the most important parts of his life.

Peter beautifully expressed his troubled feelings in the very last piece he composed, Symphony No. 6 in B minor (also known as the *Pathétique*).

He did seem to find happiness, though, composing music about love. Some of the most beautiful love music ever written can be heard in Tchaikovsky's *Romeo and Juliet* overture and in his ballet *Sleeping Beauty*.

A scene from *Sleeping Beauty*, as performed by the English National Ballet at the London Coliseum

A scene from *The Nutcracker*, as performed by the New York City Ballet

Peter Tchaikovsky lived to be fifty-three years old. Probably one of the most important things he gave to his music was beautiful and interesting melodies. A melody is the tune—the part of a musical piece that's easiest to remember. It's usually the part that's most fun to hum or whistle. Two of Peter Tchaikovsky's best loved pieces, Violin Concerto in D Major and Piano Concerto No. 1 in B-flat Minor, are filled with beautiful melodies.

It's pretty easy to find Peter Tchaikovsky's music online and on classical radio stations. During the holiday season, many ballet companies across the country put on performances of *The Nutcracker*.

LEARN MORE BY TAKING THE TCHAIKOVSKY QUIZ!

(ANSWERS ON THE NEXT PAGE.)

1. When Peter Tchaikovsky was four years old, he composed a song with the help of his three-year-old sister, Aleksandra. What did they name their piece?
- a *California Dreamin'*
- b *Our Mama in St. Petersburg*
- c *Dust in the Wind*

2. TRUE OR FALSE: When Tchaikovsky's ballet *The Nutcracker* was first performed in St. Petersburg in 1892, it was an instant hit. People bought thousands of hand-painted nutcrackers, parents decorated their children's rooms with nutcracker wallpaper, and the sale of nutcracker action figures went through the roof!

3. During his travels, Peter Tchaikovsky met many of the world's greatest composers. Who were some of them?
- a Johannes Brahms, Edvard Grieg, Gustav Mahler
- b Antonin Dvořák, Camille Saint-Saëns, Nikolai Rimsky-Korsakov
- c Stephen Foster, George Gershwin, Woody Guthrie

4. When Peter was first studying music, he became acquainted with a group of five important men known as The Mighty Handful. Who were The Mighty Handful?
- a A group of Russian Superheroes
- b Five Russian musicians and composers
- c Five of Russia's mightiest Olympic weightlifters

5. The powerful ruler of Russia, Tsar Alexander III, appreciated music, especially Tchaikovsky's music. In 1883, the tsar honored Peter by:
- a Naming a bridge after him
- b Erecting a 50-foot marble statue of Tchaikovsky
- c Awarding him with a national medal of honor

33

ANSWERS

1. b In 1844, Peter and his little sister wrote a song to honor their mother. They called their song *Our Mama in St. Petersburg*.

2. FALSE Actually, when *The Nutcracker* premiered, people weren't all that impressed. Even though the audience enjoyed Tchaikovsky's music, they thought the story was boring and didn't work very well. Some critics found fault with the set designs and thought the dancers were out of shape! Today, most people would agree *The Nutcracker* is one of the best ballets ever!

3. a and b Even if you're not familiar with the names of some of these composers, you've probably heard their music in some of your favorite movies and TV shows. If you check their music out, you'll see why Peter Tchaikovsky was inspired by these great composers.

4. b The Mighty Handful were a group of composers and musicians who wanted Russia to have its own national-sounding music. They encouraged Russian composers to use more local folk music in their compositions, and move away from music influenced by European composers. Peter agreed with some of the group's goals, but was careful to always follow his own special style.

5. c Tsar Alexander III *really* loved Tchaikovsky's music. He had Peter write music for special occasions, presented him with an important medal, and even gave him a yearly allowance.